Retur
time
and /

IMAGES OF ENGLAND

IOO YEARS OF
SCOUTING

05/08

IMAGES OF ENGLAND

100 YEARS OF
SCOUTING

STEVEN HARRIS

TEMPUS

First published 2008

Tempus Publishing
Cirencester Road, Chalford,
Stroud, Gloucestershire, GL6 8PE
www.thehistorypress.co.uk

Tempus Publishing is an imprint of The History Press Ltd

British Library Cataloguing in Publication Data.
A catalogue record for this book is available from the British Library.

ISBN 978 0 7524 4569 4

Typesetting and origination by The History Press Ltd
Printed in Great Britain

Contents

Acknowledgements

Sincere thanks are expressed to the many people, organisations and institutions who provided help with this book.

Help with advice and photographic images is particularly appreciated from the following:

Picture the Past and North East Midland Photographic Record/Heanor Library; Nick Tomlinson; The Scout Association; The British Library; Luton and Bedfordshire Local Studies Library; Bill Wendes MBE; Charterhouse School; Steven Williams and Slapstick Design Partnership; Mercers' Company Archives; Suzanne Sieger; Nigel Cole; Sally Tregaskes and 1st Par Scout Group; Christopher Vernon; East Sussex Express; Jacky and Doug Wallace; Doug Ramsey; John Mackintosh and 1st Godstone Scout Group; Norman Plastow; Richard Ivens and Roger Starr; 1st Portishead Scout Group; John F. Rickard; Geoff Rhodes; David Jones and The Perse School, Cambridge; George Tyson and Rose Hill School; 1st Wallington Scout Group; Tenth (Scottish) Finchley Scout Group; Dr Stephan Schrolkamp; 1st East Putney Scout Group; Marlborough College; 8th Hendon Scout Group; Chigwell School; Alan Shrimpton and Bryanston School; Tony Allen; Glen Webb; Michael J Allen.

Introduction

2007 was celebrated as the centenary of Scouting; quite right too! From that now famous experimental camp on Brownsea Island in August 1907, when the famous heroic soldier, Baden-Powell, tried out his ideas for scouting and citizenship training for boys, there sprang a published boys' handbook and a brand new movement.

The handbook, *Scouting for Boys*, and the Boy Scout Movement both came into life from January 1908. It was this special year that saw the growth of what was to become a twentieth-century youth phenomenon. Indeed, a world-wide youth movement with its Founder being famous for starting the movement of bare-knees, baggy shorts, big hats and broom-carrying Boy Scouts, rather than a military hero of the Boer War. In essence, 'B-P', as Baden-Powell was popularly known, became a hero twice over.

The year 1908 has a huge significance for the Scout Movement. It was only then that a Boy Scout office was set up, *Scouting for Boys* was published in parts and soon after as a complete handbook. Additionally, it was 1908 when the first uniforms and badges could be purchased, and a Scout's weekly paper was launched. *The Scout* was eagerly awaited each week by boys up and down the country, collected from the newsagent and avidly read. It remained as a weekly paper until the 1960s.

It is 2008 and the years around that date that will see many present-day Scout Groups celebrating their own unique centenaries, for many of the first troops, founded in humble conditions though exciting times, are still thriving 100 years on. To these – Baden-Powell's pioneers – and those who followed, let's salute them and the man who made it all possible!

This book, then, gives a unique pictorial record of British Scouting as it evolved during its first 100 years. Many of the photographs were taken by unknown individual members of the movement. In contrast to the many official – sometimes rather contrived – photographs of Scouting activities, many of the photographs in this book provide us with a new and genuine flavour of what many thousands of adults and boys enjoyed doing on troop night, at camp, in the park or by the river.

Be it during the early decades of the twentieth century, when Scouting was novel and often considered a sport, or more recent times, its appeal is still strong. Stars such as comedians Matt Lucas and Harry Hill were once members of the movement, along with Lord Attenborough, Sir Richard Branson, tennis player Andy Murray and footballers Michael Owen and David Beckham.

Key Scouting Dates

1857	Robert Stephenson Smyth Baden Powell, Scouting's Founder, born in London, 22 February.
1907	August – Baden-Powell's experimental camp on Brownsea Island.
1908	January – *Scouting for Boys* starts publication in fortnightly parts.
	April – *The Scout* weekly paper is launched.
	August – Baden-Powell's second Scout camp is held at Humshaugh, near Hexham.
1909	August – Baden-Powell's Sea Scout camp for 100 Scouts at Hamble, Southampton.
	September – First National Scout Rally, at the Crystal Palace, London.
1910	Girl Guide Movement founded by Baden-Powell and his sister Agnes.
1911	Windsor rally/review by the King.
1912	January – Royal Charter of Incorporation for the Boy Scouts.
	October – Marriage of Baden-Powell to Olave St Clair Soames.
1916	Wolf Cubs officially launched.
1917	Rover Scout scheme started.
1919	July – Gilwell Park near Epping Forest officially opened.
1920	July – First World Jamboree held at London's Olympia; Baden-Powell declared Chief Scout of the World.
1929	July – Arrowe Park 'Coming of Age' jamboree held in Birkenhead.
1932	October – First of Ralph Reader's gang shows.
1941	Baden-Powell, Scouting's Founder, dies in Kenya on 8 January.
	Air Scout branch launched.
1946	Senior Scouts started.
1949	Bob-a-Job fundraising scheme started.
1957	9th World Jamboree held at Sutton Coldfield.
1961	July – Baden-Powell House and hostel, South Kensington, London opened by HM The Queen.
1962	The National Trust purchased Brownsea Island for the public.
1966	June – The Chief Scout's *Advance Party Report* published: major changes in uniform, terminology and training programme.
1967	Diamond Jubilee of Scouting.
1971	New purple world membership badge introduced.
1977	June – Olave Lady Baden-Powell, World Chief Guide, dies.
1982	New younger section, 'Beavers', introduced.
1990	Girls could be permitted into the younger Scout sections if Scout groups wished.
2000	May – Millennium Camps held throughout the UK.
2002	Launch of new uniforms, sections and training programmes.
	September – Former *Blue Peter* presenter, Peter Duncan, invested as the new (ninth) Chief Scout.
2007	Centenary of the Scout Movement. Many celebrations, including World Centenary Jamboree at Hylands Park, Chelmsford, Essex, England.

one

Scouting's Founder

Scouting's Founder was christened Robert Stephenson Smyth Baden Powell. He was born near Paddington, London to Henrietta and the Reverend Professor Baden Powell on 22 February 1857. He would not be known as Robert until after the birth of the Scout Movement, at home he was commonly known by the name Stephe, which was pronounced 'Steevie'. The hyphenation of Baden to Powell would not occur until several years after his father's death, for Stephe would sadly lose his father when aged just three.

Baden-Powell saw his rise in prominence after he had left Charterhouse School and joined the army, where he proved to be a popular and charismatic figure. He was destined to spend thirty-four years in the army (and thirty-four years as leader of the Scout Movement), but he made his fame as 'Baden-Powell the heroic defender of Mafeking', during his time in the war in South Africa – 1899-1900. It was through defending the people of Mafeking and keeping the Boer fighters at bay for 217 days that the elderly Queen Victoria and British public read with a mix of apprehension and excitement the exploits of Col. Baden-Powell and his men. He became famous throughout the land and empire.

Above left: Baden-Powell aged around fifteen.

Above right: Baden-Powell at Mafeking.

Above and below: Baden-Powell's former school, Charterhouse, 1870s and modern day.

Above: Relief of Mafeking celebrations in London.

Left: Baden-Powell and Olave Soames, his soon-to-be bride, aboard the *Arcadian*, 1912.

The first photograph of
us together, on board
the "Arcadian"
Jan. 1912

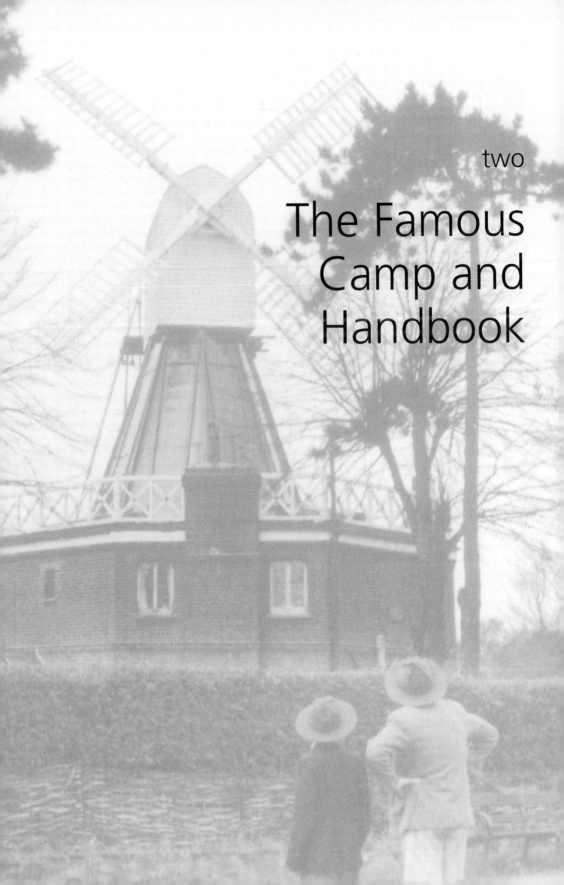

two

The Famous Camp and Handbook

Baden-Powell returned to England after the war in South Africa with concerns for the nation's young. Like others, he read reports and saw for himself just how many boys were unfit, wasting their money on cigarettes, taking blind-alley jobs and generally loafing around. They needed guidance and encouragement. Youth provision centered mainly on cadets, lads'/boys' clubs and the various boys' brigades. Influenced by this provision and also the writings and ideas of others, Baden-Powell began to formulate a scheme that would utilise aspects of current youth schemes but would be fine-tuned to incorporate his own unique ideas on citizenship training and – something he had largely taught himself whilst serving abroad – scouting. Through scouting, Baden-Powell felt that boys could develop character in a fun and purposeful way. It was not about military training, such as marching and shooting, but centered around observation, tracking, camping out and woodcraft: skills that weren't being taught at home or in schools, and all leading to independence, a sense of self-worth, and an awareness of and responsibility to others, one's country and empire.

Baden-Powell's name carried a lot of weight, he remained hugely popular as the Hero of Mafeking for a considerable period after his success in May 1900, meeting many well known people. It was in 1906, however, that a meeting with wealthy newspaper proprietor Sir Arthur Pearson spurred him on to write a scouting book specially for boys – not an army book like his well-known *Aids to Scouting* – but a unique book for boys. It would be called *Scouting for Boys*, and was published, in serial form first, in January 1908.

But Pearson also encouraged Baden-Powell to try out his boy scouting ideas by running a boys' camp. This he did in August 1907, after receiving permission from the owners of an island off Poole, in Dorset. The affluent Mr and Mrs Charles van Raalte proved keen to allow the famous soldier to run his 'boys' encampment' on Brownsea Island. They were the ideal hosts – very amenable but discrete when necessary – with good local contacts, staff and facilities. Not that Baden-Powell required many facilities: most were natural and ideal – quiet areas away from the island castle; lakes, the sea and beaches, firewood, thickets.

The ideas pioneered at Baden-Powell's camp were unusual and daring for the day. The twenty boys were a mix of the social classes: public-school boys and local town lads from the Boys' Brigade. Camping in itself was an unusual activity in those days, let alone wearing shorts and living in boy patrols. But learning about first-aid, observation, fitness, tracking and many other activities, along with the nightly camp fires, made the nine days or so into an amazing holiday. The boys and leaders little realised that they were making history in 1907, being the world's first-ever Boy Scouts.

The windmill on Wimbledon Common. It was in the cottage next to the windmill, Mill House, where Baden-Powell stayed and wrote some of the drafts for his handbook *Scouting for Boys*, in 1907.

Above: The front cover of Part 5. Who was he? What was he looking at? Where could you get hold of the uniform? Little could anyone have realised that the parts, published as a complete handbook in May 1908, would become a world bestseller.

Opposite above: The actual campsite of Baden-Powell's experimental camp of August 1907. Locals were quite familiar with the names Baden-Powell and Scout before any ideas of a Scout camp had been thought of. With Baden-Powell still being a popular topic several years after the relief of Mafeking, the *Poole Herald* of September 1904 mentioned Baden-Powell's mother under its 'Personal Gossip' column. Two years later, in not-so-far-away Salisbury, a new motor-car manufacturer advertised The Scout. It was apparently a '20hp noiseless and very springy' model.

The actual campsite where it all started.

Participants of the Brownsea camp using stones to practise marksmanship.

Brownsea Island today. Owned by the National Trust, and open to the public for much of the year, Scouts and Guides still enjoy special camping rights on the island.

Above: These two photographs depict Scouts at a 1912 rally demonstrating very similar things to what the Brownsea boys were shown. Ideas from Baden-Powell's first camp and the contents of *Scouting for Boys* were followed religiously by Scouts all over Britain.

The commemorative stone was unveiled in 1967 by Baden-Powell's daughter, the Hon. Mrs Betty Clay CBE. Sculpted by Don Potter, he also sculpted the statue of Scouting's Founder that stands outside Baden-Powell House.

Visiting Dutch Scouts in 2004.

GEN. BADEN.POWELL AND HON ODO AND MRS VIVIAN AT "GLANRAFAN" NOV. 1907.

A rare photograph of Baden-Powell taken during his lecture tour. Following the success of the Brownsea camp, in the autumn Baden-Powell embarked on a nationwide lecture tour to promote his scheme of character and citizenship training for boys.

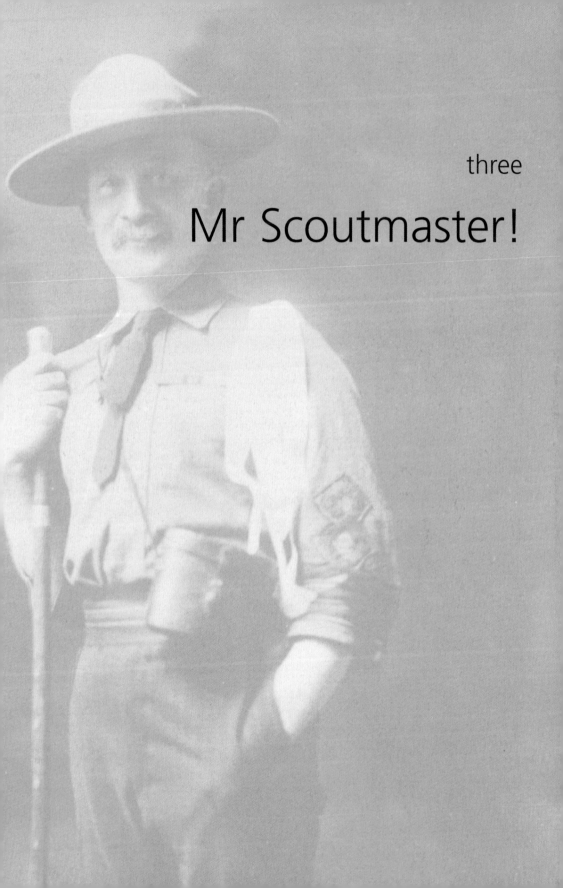

three

Mr Scoutmaster!

As soon as the parts of *Scouting for Boys* came out, many boys wanted to form their own Scout Patrols or even Troops. What they needed was an older person to become their Scoutmaster: that would make it all 'right and proper'. Older brothers, uncles, curates and Sunday school officers could all find themselves being persuaded to become a Scoutmaster. It was all so easy – or apparently so, according to the eager boys and the words in the handbook – the scheme had been designed to be very flexible and without any burdensome red tape. Prospective Scoutmasters merely had to keep one step ahead of the boys by reading the relevant chapters in the book. Of course, if they were any good at making canoes, building bridges or lassoing runaway horses, well that would be even better.

Fortunately, many men, even though most were without the skills mentioned above, were captivated by the handbook and saw great potential in the scheme. Often it was the men who proposed the idea of starting a troop to the boys. Scouting had a social, moral and religious framework. With so few outlets for boys, Scouting could be used to keep boys off the streets, to hone their skills and direct them away from blind-alley jobs, and also encourage them to keep their connections with the church.

Some new Scoutmasters, like a few of the boys themselves, did not last long. In a minority of cases problems of commitment or such things as the novelty factor played a part, resulting in some quick exits. Apart from the introduction of simple qualifying tests for Scoutmasters in late 1908, there was no widespread formal Scoutmaster training until after Gilwell Park was purchased as a training school and campsite in 1919.

Scoutmasters came from all walks of life: vicars and curates, high-street tradesmen (for example, the local tailor), some professional men, and a few with military connections. With the Boys' Brigade and Church Lads' Brigade having been well established by the time of the Scout Movement's arrival, it wasn't unknown for some brigade leaders to defect or at least assist with Boy Scout training.

Terms such as Scoutmaster and Cub Mistress (the latter not an official title anyway) became obsolete after the great changes in 1966. Publication of the Chief Scout's *Advance Party Report* was a watershed for the movement, with uniform, training and terminology all changing dramatically. 'Scoutmaster' became Scout Leader, but Scouts (no longer called Boy Scouts) often called their Scout Leaders 'Skip'. In earlier decades it had usually been a more formal 'Mr' or 'sir'.

Photo BY
KATE PRAGNELL.

Sir Baden = Powell

This page and overleaf:
Baden-Powell,
the world's first
Scoutmaster. In the
adjacent photo is
Danny Chapman,
Scoutmaster of the
1st Par Scout Troop
in Cornwall, in 1908.
He was one of the
earliest Scoutmasters
to follow in Baden-
Powell's footsteps.

The extract below is from a 1911 report that outlined the progress and development of the 1st Petersfield Scout Troop. It can be seen that such troops provided much more than mere once-a-week entertainment or semi-military training (which are ideas critics of the movement liked to propagate):

- Every Scout has been served with uniform and equipment at a cost of 18s 6d per Scout to which they contribute personally 12s 6d in 12 monthly instalments.

- During the autumn and winter months the Scout Room has been open five evenings a week, instruction being given in First Aid, Signalling, Map Reading and Shorthand. Gymnastics and Swedish Drill on Monday evenings in the Drill Hall. Outdoor games and football matches took place on Thursday and Saturday afternoons.

- A Bugle Band was formed.

- Bible classes on Sunday afternoons for boys who do not attend elsewhere.

- A Library was started with 100 books.

- Lord Selborne consented to the Troop being known as 'The Earl of Selborne's Own.'

- The Troop attended the Royal Review, Windsor on July 6th and were inspected by the King.

- The Troop took part in street collecting and a procession for Hospital Sunday Fund.

A newly formed Troop of 1908.

Above: Camberwell Troop; all becoming part of the craze that swept the country.

Opposite: An early registration form. Some troops, however, functioned for several years without registering themselves.

ASSOCIATION RETURNS.

Name of Association _Richmond Kew + Petersham_ In County of _Surrey_

Association area _From Kew Bridge to Ham - Surrey_

Comprising the Parishes of Richmond Kew + Petersham

President _George Cave Esq M.P. K.C. D.L. J.P._

Chairman _I. D. Stuart Smith Esq_

Address _Church Road. Richmond. Surrey_

Hon. Sec. _Rev Claude Beckwith M.A._

Address _Winton House. Richmond Surrey_

Date when formed _March 1910_ Date of Warrant _February 1910_

DETAILS OF ASSOCIATION.

No. of Troops.	No. of S.M.'s.	No. of A.S.M.'s and Instructors.	Total Scouts on Strength.
Six	8	9	203

SPECIAL BADGES.

Bronze Medals.	Silver Medals.	Badges of Merit.	Silver Wolves.	King's Scouts.	Cyclist Scouts.	Total.
≠	1	1	8	48	58

Signed _Claude Beckwith_

Association Secretary.

N.B.—The rules binding Associations are those in the Boy Scout Regulations. If additional bye-laws are desired a duplicate set must be attached to this Form (B) when sent to the County Secretary, in order that they may receive the approval of the Chief Commissioner at Headquarters.

Details of troops registered by Association are kept by the Association Secretary for his own information.

Photographic studios, like many other businesses, enjoyed the custom of Scouts and Scout troops.

A modern lady Scouter of 2004.

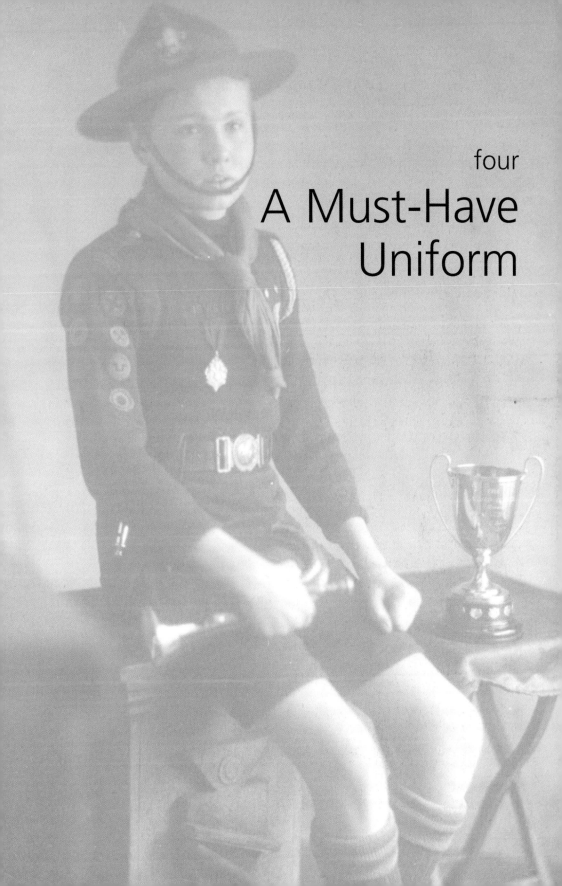

four

A Must-Have Uniform

Originally the Scout uniform of 1908 had been very minimal. In time it would develop into a Scouting trademark and be associated with smartness and parades, where eagerly sought-after patrol points could be earned and, when outdoors, good PR encouraged. But Scouting was originally intended to be an addition to existing boys' organisations' programmes – something to spice up the Boys' or Church Lads' Brigades. They already had distinctive uniforms, so if boys wanted to set up their own independent Scout patrols and troops, the suggested uniform was intended to be cheap so as not to deter poorer boys from joining.

In the first year or so, many boys made their own uniforms or adapted what they already owned. Cricket tops, for example, were used (as in the photo of early Boy Scouts in Richmond Park). This was despite the white colour, which was not good Scouting practice. Ex-Boer War hats were procured from the Army & Navy Stores, clothing was often dyed, and longs cut down into shorts. The magical stave, marked off in feet and inches – so that a Boy Scout could vault walls, test the depth of rivers, and keep hostile crowds back – normally started life as a plain broomstick.

Despite shorts being unpopular with some older Scouts later on, in the early decades boys were attracted to the movement precisely because of the uniform. They associated it with 'Baden-Powell, the Hero of Mafeking', and tended to hanker after such things as the big hat and stave. Even more so the numerous uniform accessories: knife, lanyard, water bottle and whistle.

Within a few years the Scout Movement became a big commercial concern, with many outside businesses eager to profit from it. Scout equipment, diaries and stationery, clothing, books and a host of souvenirs were all produced by the movement and by outside enterprises. With the movement becoming the largest youth movement in Britain in just a few years, the uniform range was able to expand and cater for different tastes and pockets. For example, the uniform top could be a jersey or shirt, with or without pockets and collars, and came in a range of colours and qualities.

With the major changes that arrived soon after the publication of the then Chief Scout's – Sir Charles Maclean's – *Advance Party Report* in 1966, which included making the original handbook *Scouting for Boys*, obsolete, the traditional image of the bare-kneed Boy Scout refused to disappear. Even decades after the original uniform was replaced and the term Boy Scout was dropped, both were used unofficially in the media and society

The thinking behind the original uniform was to make it as useful as possible. Thus, the big hat could be used to carry water, or as a container to feed horses. It also kept the sun and rain off. The garter tabs were probably used more for decoration rather than for their original intention of being spare darning material. The scarf, on the other hand, could serve as a cravat, bandana, triangular bandage, filter for impure water and binding material for wounds, or stretcher bearers.

There would be many other uniform reviews and changes. For example, headwear was abolished for all members (apart from Sea Scouts) in 1989. But from its earliest days, boys and leaders have always been a mix of those who loved the uniform and those who hated it, or parts of it. 2002 would see the next major shake-up of training programme and uniform. Since 2002 the colour of shirt for Scouts has been teal green, and with other items such as trousers there has been a more flexible approach (by this time a proportion of the Scouts being girls as well, the movement accepting girls since the 1990s).

Taken from a local Scout paper, the photo is of February 1908, thus a very early record of Boy Scout activity (Richmond Park).

Some of these allotment boys were the sons of south London costers, but they were also keen members of the Scout Movement.

Left: Proud, loyal and keen! Scouting gave many boys a sense of purpose in life.

Below: Advert from 1929 jamboree programme.

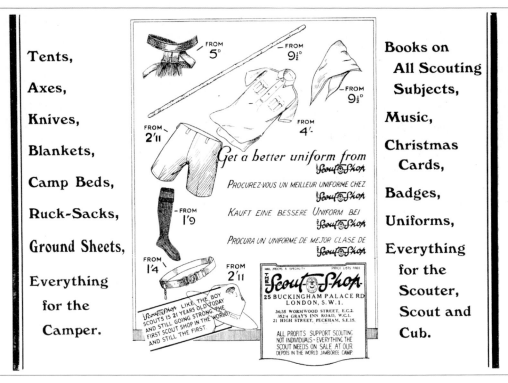

Tents,
Axes,
Knives,
Blankets,
Camp Beds,
Ruck-Sacks,
Ground Sheets,
Everything
for the
Camper.

Get a better uniform from *Scout Shop*

PROCUREZ-VOUS UN MEILLEUR UNIFORME CHEZ *Scout Shop*

KAUFT EINE BESSERE UNIFORM BEI *Scout Shop*

PROCURA UN UNIFORME DE MEJOR CLASE DE *Scout Shop*

MAIL ORDERS A SPECIALITY   PRICE LISTS FREE

THE *Scout Shop*
25 BUCKINGHAM PALACE RD
LONDON, S.W.1.

34/35 WORMWOOD STREET, E.C.2.
35/34 GRAY'S INN ROAD, W.C.1.
21 HIGH STREET, PECKHAM, S.E.15.

ALL PROFITS SUPPORT SCOUTING
NOT INDIVIDUALS - EVERYTHING THE
SCOUT NEEDS ON SALE AT OUR
DEPOTS IN THE WORLD JAMBOREE CAMP

Scout Shop LIKE THE BOY
SCOUTS IS 21 YEARS OLD TODAY
AND STILL GOING STRONG THE
FIRST SCOUT SHOP IN THE WORLD
AND STILL THE FIRST

Books on
All Scouting
Subjects,
Music,
Christmas
Cards,
Badges,
Uniforms,
Everything
for the
Scouter,
Scout and
Cub.

Above left: A St George's Day parade in Stevenage, 1967. In the autumn of that year, Boy Scout shorts were phased out.

Above right: All change! According to some, Scouting needed to take a new direction and modernise.

Dutch Scouts mixing with English Scouts, 1962.

15th Finchley Scout Group, all in the 'modern' uniform of the 1970s.

Beavers became the movement's youngest section. Even younger than Cubs, they were introduced for boys aged six to eight in 1982.

Scouts from Carmarthenshire, 2006, trying for the angler badge.

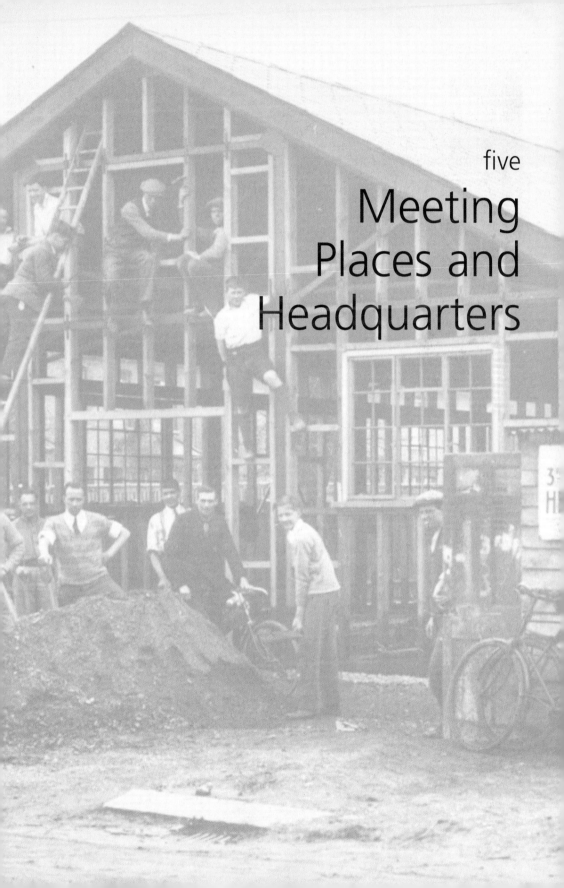

five

Meeting Places and Headquarters

In 1908 Baden-Powell offered his Scouting scheme to existing boys' organisations. It was partly designed to augment these existing organisation's programmes, many of which had marching and drill at their core. Baden-Powell's notion of Scouting consisted of citizenship training but in a fun way that exploited boys' natural instinct to form themselves into gangs, often with an older boy in charge. Thus, Scout patrols would be encouraged to learn about helping others (the good-turn), tracking, observation, first-aid and looking after one's self when camping out.

It is debatable as to what extent Scouting's Founder originally envisaged his scheme becoming a new fully-fledged independent movement. But that is what it became, boys themselves really started the Scout Movement. Although the YMCA and other organisations started their own Scout patrols and troops, Scout patrols came into existence that were completely independent and unattached to any existing organisation or institution. In a wave of excitement and urgency, across Britain boys were caught up in something akin to a new religion. If they'd been successful in coercing an adult to become their Scoutmaster, all that was needed was a meeting place.

Scouting was like a sport, it was supposed to be a game, notably a game played outdoors. So it was easy to agree a meeting place, often under a lamp post or at a secret rendezvous. Patrol calls and secret signals were the order of the day and very much part of the fun for the country's first Boy Scouts as they congregated for the weekly meeting, eager to get out and put the handbook into action.

Of course, the handbook *Scouting for Boys* also detailed instructors and boys on specific training and tests. Some sort of indoor accommodation was needed, particularly as winter set in. Additionally, storage would be required for the troop's burgeoning array of equipment: tracking irons, rope, band instruments, punch bags. If really go-ahead and successful, trek-carts and camp equipment would need a dry spot too.

Whilst the Church Lads' Brigade, schools and churches, in some instances, allowed Scouts to share their premises, a great range of Scout headquarters came into existence, often loaned by generous patrons. Stable lofts where Scouts could also practise lowering distressed victims down rickety ladders, to crypts, railway arches and old hulks were all used.

Slowly but surely Scout headquarters evolved from rented accommodation to ex-YMCA war huts, and from glorified wooden shacks with dim gas lighting to the more sophisticated brick-built affairs commonly seen after the Second World War. By this time, with the concept of the 'Scout Group', which could consist of one or more Cub packs, Scout troops, senior Scouts and Rovers, a Scout group's headquarters was often in use most nights of the week. Those still in rented accommodation belonging to someone else, although often enjoying reduced rents, did not have the luxury of being able to store much equipment or leave things out or permanently on display. Moreover, they were in competition for space and time with other users of the premises.

Martello Tower, Shorncliffe, one of numerous other unusual meeting places for Scouts. It is often forgotten that it was in the Scout headquarters – through the troop library – that many Scouts were given privileged access to a range of books to read and borrow.

An interior of a Scout headquarters. In this example the Scoutmaster wanted to remove any military connotations, the fireplace was intended to be the focal point where stories, singsongs and prayers could be enjoyed.

A new headquarters going up in 1929, and still functioning as a Scout headquarters today.

A modern Scout and Guide headquarters.

Gate entrance to the 1st Godstone's purpose-built headquarters. Constructed in the 1930s by members of the Scout Group themselves, this building on Godstone Green comprises of materials emanating from a range of different sources. It includes brickwork from Waterloo Bridge and the Houses of Parliament, ships' timbers, and twelfth-century Purbeck stone from a church in Avon.

Above and opposite: Reports of the building of this Scout headquarters reached the national press not only of Britain but Australia and America too.

Above and below: Despite their lovely meeting place, the 1st Godstone were very go-ahead. Often out and about, they can be seen here trying their hand at film making.

six

Something for the Girls

Scouting is coeducational in the UK today (and also in other countries though not all). Back in 1907 there were more distinct lines of social class and gender. In state schools boys and girls entered the building using separate entrances; some lessons were designed to cater for what those in power perceived to be the pupils' different future needs: boys were taught handicraft, girls learnt cooking and embroidery. In truth, it wouldn't have occurred to Baden-Powell to offer Scouting as a mixed activity - he wouldn't have got away with it for long anyway. Perhaps more importantly, Scouting was something unique for boys, and was especially designed to capture those who were hanging around on street corners or wasting their money on cigarettes and alcohol.

But some girls protested! Why were their brothers having all the fun? The daring ones made up their own Scout-like uniforms and even scouted the Scouts! A girl scout patrol had even brazenly turned up at the movement's first Scout rally, held at Crystal Palace in 1909. They, too, had read *Scouting for Boys* with awe and excitement.

To keep the Scouts as the intended article, a unique boys' club that exploited the natural instinct of boys to socialise and operate in gangs (patrols), Baden-Powell eventually started a separate scheme for the girls. With the help of his sister Agnes, the Girl Guide Movement was launched in 1910.

HM The Queen, who was a keen Ranger Guide. Later, a royal connection would be maintained through Prince Andrew joining the Cubs.

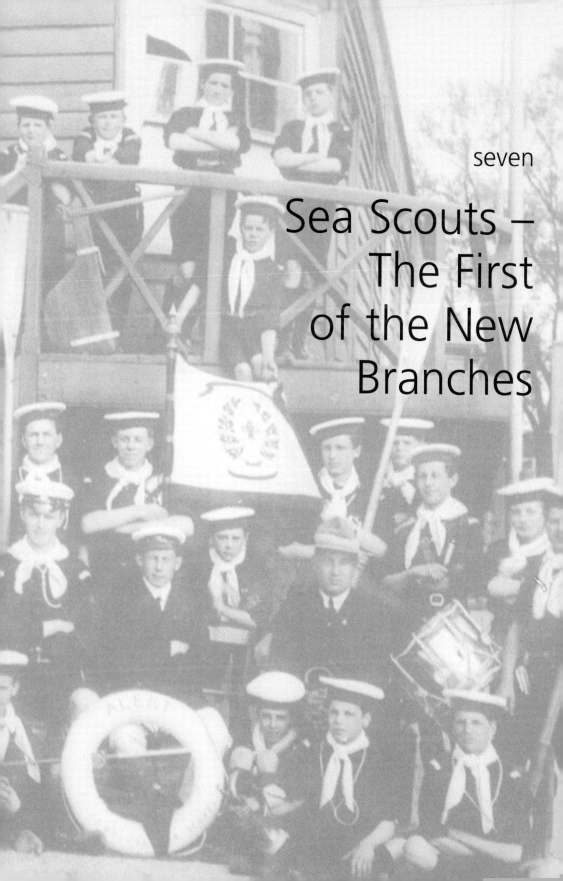

seven

Sea Scouts –
The First
of the New
Branches

Scouting was an incredibly flexible scheme, which partly explains why it became so popular and grew to the extent that it did. It did not recruit boys from only one religion or denomination; and in time boys from all classes enjoyed Scouting. Scout troops were run in poor parts of cities, in villages and towns, and also in schools, including ordinary schools, schools for handicapped children, and public schools. Eton College was one of the first public schools to take up Scouting.

But as it grew, the movement also catered for a wider age-range, Wolf Cubs and Rover Scouts, and for boys with a special interest in sea or (later on) air activities.

Scouts had swum and enjoyed boating activities as soon as Scouting was launched. Indeed, the first Boy Scouts at Baden-Powell's Brownsea Island camp had bathed and gone out in boats playing 'hunt the whale'. The movement's official Sea Scout branch, however, is generally thought to have grown from a summer camp organised by Baden-Powell in 1909. At Bucklers Hard, in Hampshire, 100 boys enjoyed a two-week camp where they spent a week on land and a week based on CB Fry's training ship, the *Mercury*. Rudyard Kipling's son, John, was a member of the camp, as was Baden-Powell's nephew, Donald.

Not long after, rules and a Sea Scout uniform came into existence. Employing family help and specialists, as he did with the Girl Guides, and later with Air Scouts, Baden-Powell got advice from his older brother, Warington. As a young man Warington had trained for sea life on HMS *Conway*. Alongside him had been Matthew Webb, who became the first person to swim the English Channel. Captain Webb became something of a superstar though later met his end by drowning whilst trying to swim across the Niagara Falls rapids. Warington, who became a KC in the Admiralty Courts, wrote a handbook for Sea Scouts.

Above: Coastguard training for Sea Scouts, off the Kent coast, *c.* 1912.

Right: From a programme for the 1913 Birmingham Scout Exhibition.

PICTURES OF THE EXHIBITION, SEA SCOUTS' DISPLAY, and RALLY,

Held in Birmingham, July 2nd-8th, 1913.

Above and left: 1st Cambridge Sea Scouts.

Headquarters of the 99th Bristol (Cabot) Sea Scouts. The main structure is a reinforced concrete grain barge which was built in 1952.

Land Scouts, too, enjoyed water activities, as seen here at Portland Bill in 1932.

A river trip near Arundel Bridge.

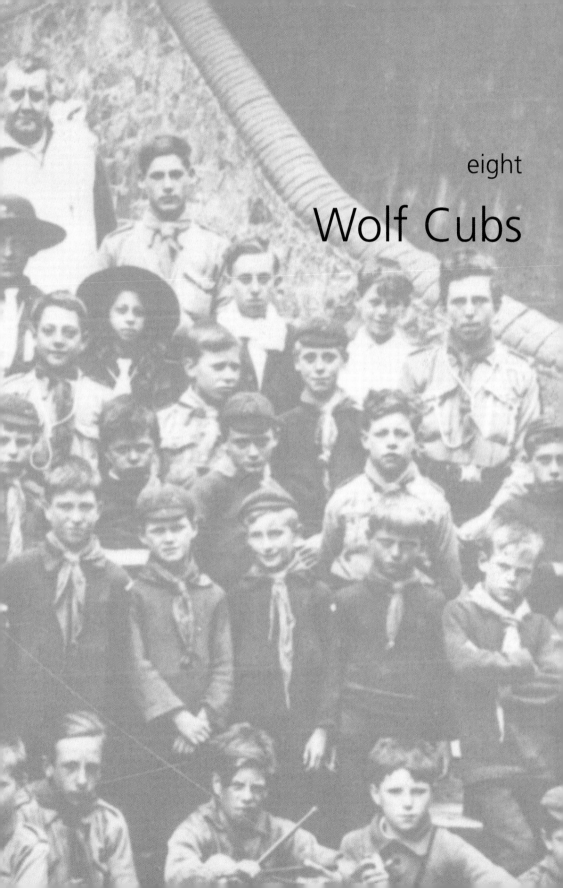

eight

Wolf Cubs

The Wolf Cub scheme was started to cater for younger boys who had been clamouring to join the Scouts. Eager as they had been, Baden-Powell was worried that allowing younger boys to do Scouting – which some Scout Troops were doing unofficially – would overtax young boys physically. More importantly, he felt it might deter older boys from joining, making it into 'kiddy Scouting', and rather lower the kudos the movement had with patrons and employers.

Officially launched in 1916, Wolf Cubs had been developed under various guises of junior Scouting since around 1911. Before being known and trialled as Wolf Cubs after 1914, they had often been known as 'Young' or 'Cadet' Scouts. Until 1928, Wolf Cub packs did not have to have any connection with a Scout troop; they were registered as entirely separate units. Nonetheless, Wolf Cub packs proved to be good feeders for Scout troops. In fact, eventually Wolf Cubs proved to be so popular that the movement had more registered Cubs than Scouts.

With the help of Rudyard Kipling's approval of the movement adapting his *Jungle Stories*, the scheme captivated many thousands of boys' imaginations. At weekly meetings they would perform the Grand Howl opening ceremony and chant 'Dyb, dyb, dyb - Do your best!' Akela, the Cubs' leader, was often a woman. Although there had been occasional female Scoutmasters – notably during the First World War – it was the launch of the Wolf Cub branch that gave many women of the early 1920s a rare and socially legitimate opportunity to leave their homes in the early evening and do something they considered fun, empowering and worthwhile.

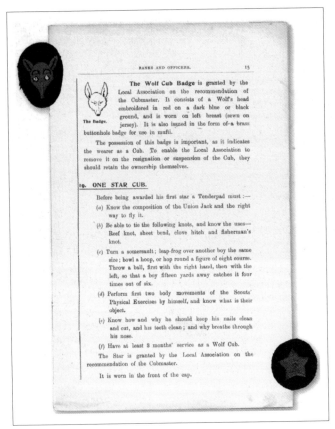

Some of the requirements for the Cubs' one- and two-star tests were far more practical and of greater use than what the boys were being taught in school.

Above and below: Wolf Cubs on holiday in Guernsey, before and after a scrub up.

Above: Knotting practice, early 1960s.

Left: Cub days at Gilwell Park rapidly grew in popularity.

BACK

TO

GILWELL ?

PACK ENTRY FOR CUB DAY, GILWELL PARK, 2nd JULY, 1966

Name of Pack

Numbers attending : Cubs   Adults   Fee enclosed

Signature of Cubmaster

Address

Are you travelling by coach—train—bus—other transport ?

Please return this completed form, TOGETHER WITH A STAMPED ADDRESSED ENVELOPE to THE CAMP CHIEF, GILWELL PARK, CHINGFORD, LONDON, E.4. A receipted card will be sent to you. Bring this with you, otherwise you will be asked to pay again ! We regret, we cannot accept little brothers and sisters in the party, and only adults actually helping with the Cubs may be included.

If your Pack is very small or very large, we leave it to you to make a suitable adjustment to the fee.

Opposite above: Presentation of a leader's warrant.

Opposite below: Sheath knives were still quite commonly worn on uniforms until the 1970s.

Above: Enrolment card.

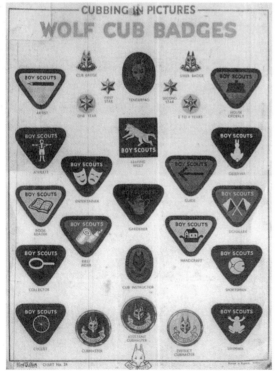

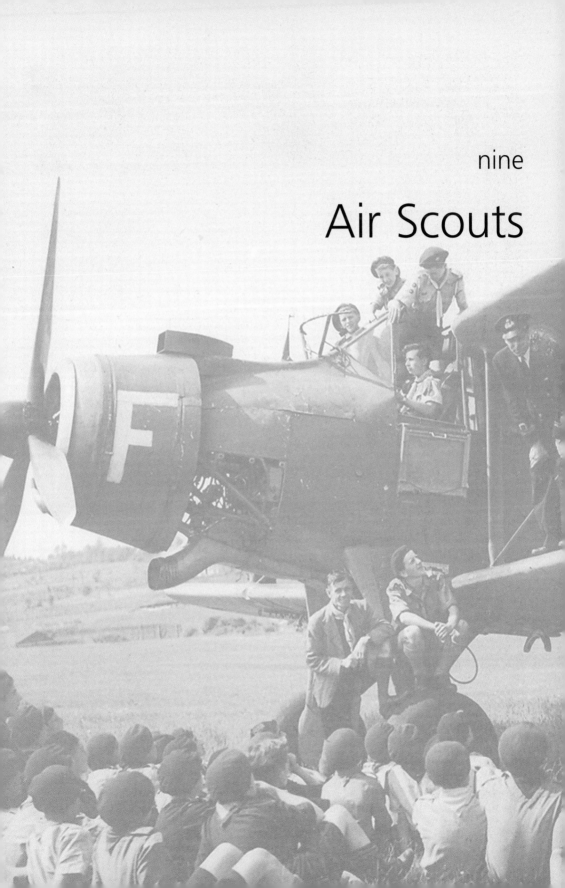

nine

Air Scouts

The Air Scout branch was a late starter for the movement, being launched in 1941 (in the same month and year Baden-Powell passed away). The Rover Scout section, for young men in the movement, had been started during the First World War, and all the other sections (bar the Senior Scouts) had been well established before this. Now although there was great interest in flying during Scouting's early days, flying was very much in its infancy. Olave Soames, later to become Baden-Powell's wife, recalls in her autobiography that in her youth, upon hearing the noise of an aircraft, people would rush out of doors and point to the sky saying 'Look! a flying machine!'

Baden-Powell himself tells us in his diary entry for July 1912 that while he was in Durban he attended an aviation display by Paton, one of the famous airmen of the early days: 'He took me up for a most enjoyable flight.' His brother Baden might have been envious. Baden Fletcher Baden-Powell was an expert in military balloons and kites, being known in the family as the balloonatic.

Scouts near aerodromes had been attending special airmanship classes during the First World War, which were designed to train them in aircraft recognition and maintenance. Baden-Powell made Baden his Scout Commissioner for Aviation in 1923, but a separate branch did not materialise at that time. Apart from Baden's early death, there were several other reasons for this. Firstly, there was the handicap of finding suitably qualified people to lead the section, but it was also felt that such a branch might lead boys away from the more basic though important essentials of Scout training.

After the advent of the RAF and the daring-do exploits of pilots during the Second World War, flying became a keen interest for many boys. Former Scout and Scout Commissioner, Guy Gibson, would lead the now-famous Dam Busters raid. He was awarded the Victoria Cross.

The government had just started an Air Cadet scheme too, so it was considered a prudent and ripe moment for the movement to launch its latest branch.

Above: Actor Laurence Olivier talking to Air Scouts at the first All England Air Scout Camp, 1942.

Opposite: 'Aero Scouts' – Boy Scouts, as a one off, were used by the Aerial League to undertake balloon despatch running at Battersea Gas Works, 1910. Baden-Powell is far left, his brother Baden is far right.

Epsom Air Scouts at Redhill, 1981.

ten

Scouting in Schools

After the start of the Scout Movement a few private schools were quick to have terms such as 'character training' and 'scouting' included in their prospectuses. Some state schools began running Scout troops, though not many did. The headmaster of Harrow County School was a keen advocate of Scouting and was well known for saying that only twenty-two boys can play in a football match, but any number can enjoy Scouting.

Orphanages (including Dr Barnardo Homes) and special schools quickly offered Scouting: it gave the boys another interest and also helped the running of the home or school. Quite a few preparatory schools, from about 1910, took up Scouting once the first one or two had started. It was relatively easy to get going in preparatory schools, in addition to having good facilities such as grounds and perhaps a swimming pool, it did not conflict with the school's Officer Training Corps (OTC, CCF today). If preparatory schools had an OTC at all, it was only for the older boys.

In public schools Scouting would not be introduced until the 1920s, and for most it would be the late 1920s. This was partly because such schools already had the sort of ethos Scouting was trying to encourage: an *esprit de corps*. It was sold to the public schools on the basis that older boys could be trained up as the Scoutmasters or commissioners of the future, thus helping to ensure a good supply of leaders – of the right sort – for the movement.

Very early on Scouts made use of night classes held in elementary schools and elsewhere for special courses to pass certain Scout tests and badges. Whilst doctors had helped with first-aid training, Boy Scouts could learn about such things as printing and basketwork at night school. Baden-Powell had intended that all the proficiency badges, in fact, should give a boy a taster and help him to see where his potential and future employment lay.

In the immediate foreground is Northbrook House (now Great Comp, or the Sanatorium). Behind it stretching diagonally to the right are Hodgsonites, Bodeites, Pageites, Robinites and Daviesites. Immediately behind the tower block and the dining rooms are Lockites and Weekites. Across Under Green are the main school buildings, with the Memorial Chapel behind.

Aerial view of Charterhouse, Baden-Powell's former school. Baden-Powell's son Peter founded the first Scout Troop at the school in 1927. Wilfrid Noyce, a former master at the school and a member of the team which climbed Everest, was a Scoutmaster at the school for eleven years.

A Cambridge county school, 1935. Cambridge Scouting benefited from good support by graduates and staff from the university (as did Oxford Scouting).

The Perse School in Cambridge was a very early starter in Scouts. It went on to have Land, Air and Sea Scout Troops within the school. Like Dulwich College and other well-known public schools, it still has an active Scout troop today. The photo depicts a winning Patrol after a camp inspection.

The Perse Troop at camp.

Before Charterhouse, Baden-Powell attended Rose Hill preparatory school in Tunbridge Wells.
After the Scout Movement had started, 'The Scouter' was a local landmark for many years, situated
as it was on the school's front lawn. The school at that time ran a Sea Scout Troop; today it still has
Cubs and Brownies.

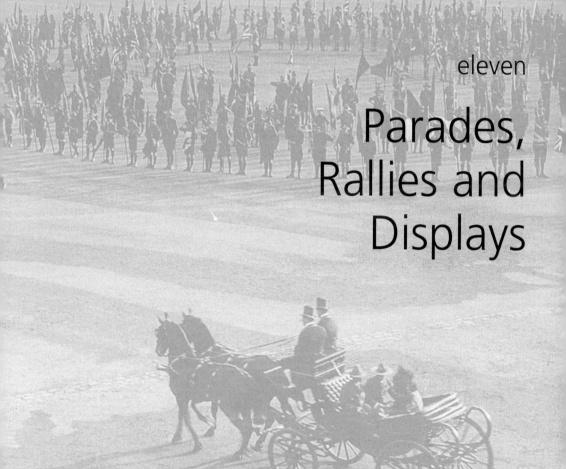

eleven

Parades, Rallies and Displays

Whereas weekly pack and troop meetings have been called just that – meetings – for decades, they were originally known as parade night. Scouts often met several times a week, one night might be set aside for games (club night), another for outdoor work or visits, so parade night was often more formal, where full uniform was expected and weekly subs were paid.

Sometimes when marching off to the local common or when off to camp, the local troop would look as though they were on some sort of parade. The Scouts could cause quite a stir as they formed up and marched off, often with bugles sounding if not a full band. Similarly, when setting off for camp, before such things became common-place activities, the whole street would know the Scouts were off to camp. With a flag in front and trek-cart wheels clattering along, intentional or not, it was a parade of Scouts.

To put themselves more officially on show, Troops would attend church parades and also district church parades. Parades evolved into Rallies, as they gave local Troops the chance to show other Troops and the general public how large, smart and efficient they were. In addition to the national Scout rallies, the first of which was held at south London's Crystal Palace in 1909, there were many local rallies held all over Britain on a regular basis. Before radio and television, such events were valuable media exercises and often well covered in the press. They also varied in style and content, however, some later turning into Scout exhibitions and displays. With fundraising in mind, fêtes and shows served as both money-earners and PR exercises, as did the Bob-a-Job scheme after 1949.

Advancing on from the district rally, parade and display became the county event: a rally or, even, Jamboree, which was not a half-day event but a weekend. The ultimate jamboree is better known as a national event lasting at least a week. They were designed for Scouts of many nations to come together in peace, sharing individual customs and cultures. Normally held every four years, the first World Jamboree was held at London's Olympia in 1920 (all others have been held outdoors), where Baden-Powell was declared Chief Scout of the World. He attended his last jamboree in 1937 though his wife, Olave, World Chief Guide, continued to attend jamborees and many other Scout and Guide functions long after her husband's death.

The most recent jamboree, coinciding with the movement's centenary, was again held in England: 2007 saw over 40,000 Scouts from countries from all over the world camp at Hylands Park, near Chelmsford, Essex.

A May rally of 1912.

A smaller rally at Burton Joyce to welcome a visit by Baden-Powell.

A huge Boy Scout rally in Hyde Park, 1914.

Opposite above: Baden-Powell on horseback at the Birmingham Exhibition, 1913.

Opposite below: Time for a break?

Best behaviour please!

Above and below: Ranmore Common annual rally of 1949. These Surrey rallies had started in 1912.

Cub Fete Day.

Come on parents! Godstone, 1930s.

These Scottish Scouts were from Finchley, London!

King Kong being readied for the Scouts' contribution to a carnival.

Above: Farnsfield Scouts perform a 'ballet' in their show of 1954.

Left: Akela getting things ready at the Milford Carnival, 1960s.

twelve

Scout
Transport

The best form of transport for the earliest Scouts was 'Shanks's pony', their legs. There was not the wide transport options of today, horse traffic, tram and rail being the chief ones, but getting around on their own two feet was both healthy and economical.

Cycling soon grew in popularity for Scouts. At the turn of the twentieth century, however, when Baden-Powell's sister took it up, the new sport of cycling was often considered a daring activity for ladies. Agnes Baden-Powell, like many other young women of her time, relished the freedom and independence bicycling afforded them.

For Scouts, the trek-cart was a remarkable troop accessory. Bulky camp equipment could be transported to camp cheaply, and items for jumble sales or salvage could be transported with relative ease. Injured persons could be carried on the troop trek-cart. Sometimes this could involve one of the troop's own members having come off worse with an unwieldy trek-cart! Handling fully loaded carts properly was almost an art form in itself.

Because the trek-cart could be dismantled, it could even be carried on trains. Scouts took their trek-carts all over Britain and even for camps in Europe. The sight of Boy Scouts going off to camp with their trek-cart, often singing a favourite troop song along the way, lasted well into the 1950s. Occasionally Scouts in the 1970s were accused of having 'petrol feet', the Scout Group minibus becoming more and more popular. On the other hand, minibuses were far safer than the common 1920s and 1930s method of bundling Scouts into the back of a lorry: often no seats, let alone seatbelts.

Early Cub transport.

The Portishead trek–cart team. Troops liked to time themselves over distances and/or compete in dismantling and reassembling trek–carts.

Mitcham Scouts of the 1950s with their 'pride and joy'.

Below: Kent Scout cyclists of the 1920s. At one stage, if a Boy Scout had earned the cyclist badge but no longer owned a bicycle, he was supposed to return the badge.

Opposite: By foot, bicycle or motor-cycle?

Baden-Powell and Olave. They were bought a car as a wedding present in 1912. In 1929, at the Arrowe Park World Jamboree, Baden-Powell was presented with a Rolls Royce. This had been purchased through Scouts each giving a penny for a present for the Founder.

Less 'health and safety' or risk assessment then.

Hinwick Scouts in Belgium, 1953.

Above and next page above: Let the train take the strain, and don't forget the pop! Before the Beeching cuts, Scouts had great access to the countryside via the train. British Rail was generally good at offering discount prices and arranging for camp kit to be forwarded on to the campsite in advance of the Scouts' arrival. There were occasions, however, when the kit did not arrive when it was supposed to.

Above: Similarly, London Scouts made good use of parents and contacts.

Opposite: The lorry was transporting Cornish Scouts for a camp at Bodmin, 1920s.

A competitor at the National Scoutcar Races, 1969. This popular event had started as the Scouts'
Soapbox Derby in 1939 at Brooklands Racetrack.

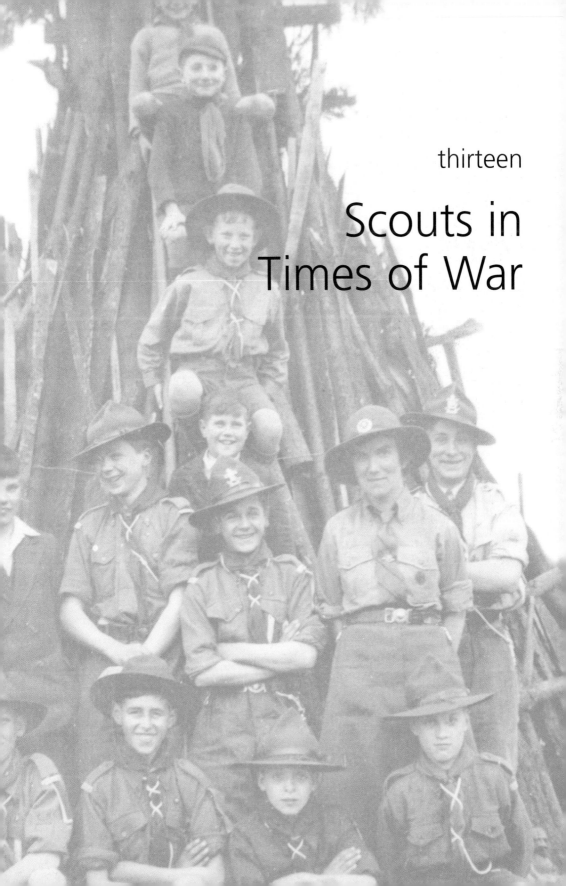

thirteen

Scouts in Times of War

I do not think I am exaggerating when I say that the young boyhood of our country, represented by the Boy Scouts Association, shares the laurels for having been prepared with the old and trusted British Army and Navy. For both proved their title to make a claim when the Great War broke upon us like a thief in the night. It is no small matter to be proud of that the Association was able within a month of the outbreak of war to give the most energetic and intelligent help in all kinds of service. When the boyhood of a nation can give such practical proofs of its honour, straightness and loyalty, there is not much danger of that nation going under, for these boys are in training to render service to their country as leaders in all walks of life in the future.

Prime Minister Lloyd George, 1917

In fact, rather than 'within a month', Boy Scouts had been able to be of service to the local authorities just days after war had been declared. With the Second World War, Scouts had helped a year earlier with fitting gas masks. And coast-watching duties, carried out by around 23,000 Boy Scouts, continued for some time after hostilities had ceased.

The kind of help provided by Boy Scouts during one or both wars included help with: sending messages, issuing call-up papers, evacuation, guarding reservoirs and railways, collecting salvage, erecting shelters, sounding the 'all clear', working on harvest camps, and hospital orderly duties.

Depending on local circumstances, many Scout activities continued during both wars. Even camping, despite rationing and the blackout, was permissible at certain times, though tents had to be camouflaged, and leaders were in very short supply.

Former boys of Cheltenham College (junior department) highlight the problems that arose, particularly when at camp, after rationing had been introduced:

Back at school Mrs Johnston, the Headmaster's wife, was an expert at disguising food 'substitutes' but at camp it was often almost impossible to cook them. Powdered egg never seemed to make anything but a thin yellow paste; powdered milk spoilt perfectly good tea; 'Smash' tasted like soap powder and a tin of Spam (Scientifically Produced Artificial Meat) just did not satisfy the hunger of a ravenous Scout Patrol. On the credit side we occasionally snared a rabbit and once at Stowell Park, a pheasant was shot with a home-made bow and arrow constructed from bamboo canes pinched from the Gardener's store!

By 1940 Baden-Powell had retired to Nyeri with Olave. He died on 8 January 1941. His body remained in his beloved Kenya, being buried in the grounds of St Peter's Church.

Across Britain church services were held, and a memorial service for the life of Baden-Powell was held in Westminster Abbey on 27 January 1941. A Baden-Powell memorial fund was set up the following year, on St George's Day, which eventually led to the building of Baden-Powell House in London's South Kensington.

Telegr : "SCOUTCRAFT, LONDON."
Teleph : 6854 GERRARD.
(2 lines).

IN REPLY PLEASE ADDRESS
THE SECRETARY,
AND QUOTE.....................

THE BOY SCOUTS ASSOCIATION,

116, VICTORIA STREET,

LONDON, S.W.

4th August, 1914.

MOBILIZATION OF BOY SCOUTS.

In this time of national emergency comes the opportunity
for the Scouts Organisation to show that it can be of material
service to the country.

The Scouts can now give valuable assistance to the State
at home - and for this their training and organisation has already
to a great extent fitted them.

Their duties would be non-military, but would in some
cases come within the scope of police work, and these would be
carried out under the general direction of the Chief Constable
in each County, where he cares to utilise the services of the
Scouts. The duties would include the following:-

(a) Handing out notices to inhabitants and other duties connected
with billeting, comandeering, warning, etc.

(b) Carrying out communications by means of despatch-riders,
signallers, wireless, etc.

(c) Guarding and patrolling bridges, culverts, telegraph lines,
etc., against damage by individual spies.

(d) Collecting information as to supplies, transport, etc., available.

(e) Carrying out organised relief measures among inhabitants.

(f) Helping families of men employed in defence duties, or sick
or wounded.

(g) Establishing First Aid, dressing or nursing stations, refuges,
dispensaries, soup kitchens, etc., in their clubrooms.

Below: War-time Scout
messengers.

Above left: Scouts used as propaganda (source uncertain).

Above right: A painting of Jack Cornwell by Frank Salisbury. He was formerly a keen east London Boy Scout, but became the 'hero of Jutland', and is believed to be the youngest Briton to win a VC. Despite receiving horrific injuries in the 1916 conflict, Cornwell remained at his post. He sadly died some days later.

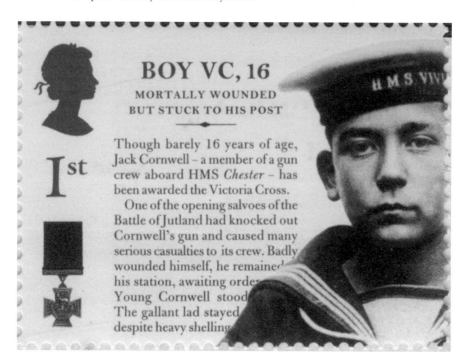

Right: Boy Scouts had been well trained before the First World War, as can be seen in this photo of a Kew Scout, fire hose at the ready in 1909.

No 3 Platoon,
Home Guard,
3 Lichfield Road,
Kew.

27th September 1940.

Dear Sir,   European War 1940.

                We are writing to thank you and the Boy Scouts
on behalf of the Volunteers Home Guard, No 3 Platoon, 3 Lichfield
Road, for the invaluable service rendered during the months of
August and September 1940 under very trying conditions during
Air Raids, by carrying rations and performing numerous other duties,
in fact they performed valuable service which has been very much
appreciated

            Signed

                 Major Commanding,
                 3 Platoon, H.G.

                    3 Lichfield Road, Kew, Surrey.

To the Scoutmaster,
Kew District.

Ref. FR/HB/Camp   MINISTRY OF FOOD

From   Newport Food   To.   Mr. S. Schaffer,
Office,   1, Faversham Road,
20, High Street,   Catford, S.E.6
Newport, I.W.

Date   26/7/50

Dear Sir, .

Boy Scouts' Camp

Further to particulars received
to-day from the Lewisham Food Office,
I have pleasure in enclosing herewith
food permits in respect of your Camp
to be held at Corfe Farm, Shalfleet,
I.W., from 30th July to 12th August,
1950.

Yours faithfully,

R. J. Grout.

for A. J. WISTAU,
Food Executive Officer.

Encs. (2)

INTERNATIONAL SCOUT'S CLUB
MARKET SQUARE

A welcome awaits you at the above club

5.p.m.-10.p.m.   Refreshments

EVERY DAY   GAMES

For members of the Scoutmovement only.

Please bring this card with you.

Introduced by _L. Stuberneyr_

19-12-44

Farnsfield Scouts celebrating the end of the war whilst in camp, 1945.

One of the millions of Boy Scouts created under Baden-Powell's scheme. Helping with civilian duties was always the order of the day, and with so many men being called up, Boy Scouts helped to fill a serious gap in manpower.

Peter, Baden-Powell's son. He had had a difficult start in life, being the son of a famous soldier and founder of the world's largest voluntary youth movement. Although less extrovert than his father, Peter did much to increase the profile of the BP Guild, a branch for older members and supporters of Scouting. Sadly, he died young, aged forty-nine.

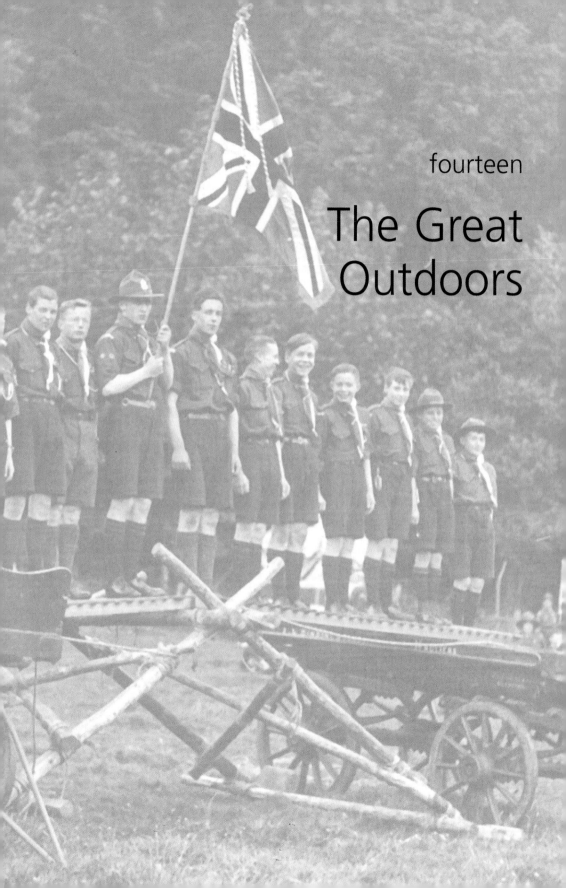

fourteen

The Great Outdoors

Until the boys have realized the call of the wild and the beauty of God's work in Nature, until they have grasped the joy of the scent of the wood smoke in their nostrils and of the deftness of camper-craft in their finger-tips, a Troop of so-called Scouts is little more than a drill brigade.

Baden-Powell, 1918

As Baden-Powell and others liked to remind Scouts and their leaders, it was important to remember the out in Scouting. Within months of being formed, troops ventured off for rambles and treks in the countryside. Pre-First World War, transport was invariably by foot or cycle, making trips out cheap and easy to plan. The first Scouts of 1908 and the years close to it, one has to remember, were true Scouting pioneers. If a Scout was attending a trip or a camp, then, often, most of the boys in the troop were doing it for the first time. They were making history in their troop: there were not likely to be any boys with much greater experience than them, and certainly no such things as Wolf Cubs or Rover Scouts.

Today such a normal activity as camping is still considered to be the number one attraction for girls and boys joining the movement. Yet in 1908 camping was considered to be a slightly quirky activity by many. Some viewed it as something of an elitist sport enjoyed by a few of the cranky middle-classes. Others equated it with the military or gypsies. Many Scouts' parents initially viewed it with a certain degree of suspicion or concern: by camping out, boys risked getting colds, rheumatism, food poisoning and, for good measure, assaulted or abducted by vagabonds.

Such worries did not last long, however, as most boys returned home with a better complexion, a full stomach, new skills and a host of interesting experiences. More importantly, a point often underestimated by social historians, throughout many decades thousands upon thousands of boys gained access to the countryside and fresh air. Such opportunities for travel, to form life-long friendships, and develop character and independence would not have come the way of many of the boys had they not joined the Scouts. This is not to disregard the special camaraderie and similar experiences enjoyed by boys in the brigades and boys' clubs, but the Scout Movement, largely due to its huge size and quickly accumulated prestige, reached a far greater number of boys. Moreover, through the Scouts boys were given easier access to camping and it occurred on a much more frequent basis. Importantly, Scout camping was very much boy-led, where boys camped in small units, patrols, and mostly cooked for and looked after themselves.

The Scout Movement gained an excellent reputation for high camping standards, but one has to feel a little sorry for some of the first Scouts who, if unlucky, found themselves waking up in collapsed tents, being flooded out or attacked by wasps. This was part of a steep learning curve for them and often their Scoutmasters too, who were not greatly experienced in such matters unless they had a military background. All too frequently the equipment was old, cumbersome and worn-out. But away from school, overcrowded homes and demanding employers, camping was a great escape.

Scout camps did not change that much for many decades. Below are memories from a former Scout of the 1st Wallington Scout Troop in the 1920s and 1930s. In the period to which these memories relate, in each class in a school, it would not have been uncommon for nearly half of the boys to have been in the Scouts.

When we went on weekend camps, each boy would be given a list of supplies he was expected to take with him ... perhaps potatoes, bread and sausages, or beans, butter and cocoa ... We all provided a share of whatever was needed, and our mothers wrapped these provisions up for us in strong paper or canvas bags.

When the Friday of one of these camps came along, I would race home from school to change into my Scout uniform. My kitbag was always kept in the cupboard under the stairs, so I would ferret it out, and load it with everything I needed - toothbrush, soap and towel, a pair of old shorts, a groundsheet, and finally (a cherished possession), my 'fleabag', a sleeping bag which my mother had made for me by sewing two blankets together. Then I'd pick up the things on my list, along with a handful of crisp Cox's orange pippins bought for me by my mother, who knew how hungry boys could get at any time, let alone when they'd been racing around in the fresh air all day! Then I would stand at the front gate, waiting for the trek-cart to come along. All the others had met on the way to Perrott's Wood, where we were to camp, and so I was picked up last, to take my place next to Les ... We had to cover seven or eight miles to Perrott's Wood, but it was all part of the fun, and we would walk with the cart, or run in sheer exuberance.

THE BOY SCOUTS. Swimming Exhibition.

In around 1910, when swimming wasn't regularly taught in schools, boys could learn 'the art' by joining the Scouts. It would not be until the 1930s when public lidos came to the fore, with around 170 being built at this time. The sea and rivers were where many of the earliest Scouts were taught this vital skill.

Swimming, the sun and fresh air, along with physical culture teams – as depicted by Scouts here – became hugely popular from the late 1920s. Scouts had had something of a head start in this area.

Above: 1st Backwell Scouts at the first Somerset Jamboree, Freshford, 1912. The Scoutmaster (far right) was Harold James, who represented Great Britain at archery in the 1908 Olympics.

Below: Whilst trek-carts were used as camp transport, this Bristol troop show that they could also be used as bridges (1931).

A rare photograph of German 'Scouts' – members of the Wandervogel youth movement rather than actual Boy Scouts – who toured Britain after a party of English Scouts had visited Germany in the same year of 1909.

Time for lunch?

Troops with a strong church attachment still found time for religious observance.

LOCKERIDGE TROOP

SUMMER CAMP AT BLANDFORD

Aug 11 to 16

Friday

Tea
Sugar
Milk
Bread
Butter
Jam

Cocoa
Biscuits
Cheese

Saturday

Quick Oats
Sugar
Milk
Tea
Kippers
Salt
Bread
Butter
Jam

Stewing steak
carrots
onions
potatoes
suet
flour
currants

Bread
Butter
Jam
Tea
Sugar
Milk

Bread
Butter
Jam
Tea
Sugar
Milk

Cocoa
Biscuits

Sunday

Force
Sugar
Milk
Tea
Eggs
Bread
Butter
Marmalade

Roast Mutton
Potatoes
Beans
Fruit salad

Tea
Sugar
Milk
Bread
Butter
Jam
Cake

Cocoa
Biscuits

Monday
Quick Oats
Sugar
Milk
Tea
Sausages
Bread
Butter
Marmalade

Hike rations
Meat pies
Apples
Chocolate
Chops
Potatoes
Onions
Flour
Fruit salad
Porridge
Tea
Sugar

Sausages

Tuesday

Salmon
Rice
Eggs
Bananas
Jellies

Wednesday

Force
Sugar
Milk
Tea
Eggs
Bread
Butter
Marmalade

A camp menu of 1934, belonging to the Marlborough College Troop.

BE PREPARED

10th St, Pancras Troop.
BOY SCOUTS ASSOCIATION.
(Incorporated by Royal Charter.)

SCOUTMASTER
C. E. Ashton.

Asst. SCOUTMASTER
E. S. Whittlestone.

Hon. SCOUTMASTERS
R. B. Fletcher.
A. E. Goldring.

Scout Headquarters,

Lewisham Road. N. W. 3

23rd May, 1924.

Reginald Bray Esq.,

Shere, Surrey.

Dear Sir,

May I again have the privilage of camping with a
party of boys from the above Troop in Coombe Bottom at
Whitsun, from Whit Saturday to Whit Monday inclusive.

You will doubtless remember giving me permission
to camp last year.

Thanking you in anticipation.

Yours faithfully,

Before telephones were commonplace, good letter writing was a great asset.

Right: Sandroyd School Scouts in camp, 1912.

The remaining photographs are all from the World Jamboree of 1937. Held in Holland, it would be the last Jamboree attended by Baden-Powell.

106

Wessel, America.

Japan.

L. F. Lee, China.

fifteen

Scout Humour

An unwritten Scout Law, well known by experienced members of the Scout Movement, was 'A Scout is not a fool'. Nonetheless, like other organisations, the Scouts have always been able to find humour in aspects of Scouting. At camp, for example, novice Scouts (Tenderfoots) often found themselves running errands to find tins of elbow grease or left-handed axes. When camp grub was served up, boys were encouraged to 'Eat it quick, before it gets dirty!'. In the 1920s it was almost inconceivable for a troop member not to have a nickname. Taffy, Lanky, Cheddar are more obvious ones, though I, as a Scout, remember one fat farm boy at camp who, even by his parents, was known as Barrel.

There have been numerous Scout cartoonists over the years, who drew for the movement's various magazines. Former Field Commissioner, John Sweet, is a popular and enduring example, whose work spanned more than six decades. Some of his work is portrayed on the following pages. But an early precedent was set for the movement by a well known commercial cartoonist producing a drawing for *Punch* magazine. Bernard Partridge (sharing Baden-Powell's initials) drew, in 1909, a helpful Boy Scout escorting 'Mrs Britannia'. This and others that followed in later years in *Punch* (also by E.H. Shepard - of *Winnie-the-Pooh* fame - and others) was quite sympathetic and without the satirical edge meted out on other subjects. After that first *Punch* cartoon, the local and national press has continued with occasional Scout cartoons up to the present day, 'Giles' being one example of not so long ago.

The traditional big-hatted Boy Scout of the 1950s, too, has often popped up in cartoons whose subject had no connection with the movement. For example, in one cartoon Boy Scouts were portrayed as ballboys at Wimbledon one year; something Boy Scouts have never been engaged in at Wimbledon. On the other hand, the ubiquitous Boy Scouts crop up in one of Alfred Wainwright's illustrations in his Lakeland Fells guidebook. Boy Scouts, along with others, have walked all over the fells and elsewhere.

Baden-Powell himself was a talented artist, one well known for being able to draw equally well with either hand; he became a member of the London Sketch Club. Indeed, at official meetings at Headquarters he could often be noticed doodling on the blotting paper; apparently there was always a rush by the office boys afterwards to collect these.

In his *Scouting for Boys* and other works, Baden-Powell devised his character Tommy the Tenderfoot who, though always keen, seemed always to be unwittingly showing everyone else precisely how not to do something. The term Tenderfoot originated from the colonies, and referred to a newcomer or greenhorn.

TOMMY THE TENDERFOOT SERIES.
No. 7.

THE SCOUTS' STAFF.

There's something that makes all the onlookers laugh,
It's Tommy again; he's forgotten his staff.

TOMMY THE TENDERFOOT SERIES.

No. 9.

THE PIONEER.

Poor Tommy's forgotten to sharpen his axe,
So the tree only suffers a series of whacks.

BOY SCOUTS
JOB
WEEK

LONDON LAUGHS ... By LEE

[No. 1,401] BOY SCOUTS' ASSOCIATION

" You buzz off before I change into civvies and punch
your nose."

PUNCH, OR THE LONDON CHARIVARI—August 4, 1920.

THE LEAGUE OF YOUTH.

WAR-WEARY WORLD (at the Jamboree). " I WAS NEARLY LOSING HOPE, BUT THE SIGHT OF
ALL YOU BOYS GIVES IT BACK TO ME."

By the courtesy of " Punch."

'Camp fire's burning, campfire's burning . . .'

'But for you and me, Akela, it's "Au Revoir", not "Goodbye".'

This page: Cartoons are all by John Sweet.

'Keep thinking of Rudyard Kipling's "If".'

sixteen

Places with a Scouting Connection

After his fame at Mafeking, Baden-Powell's name and image were used for every conceivable item, from dolls, to kettles, to board games, to cigars. Boats, roads and schools were named in his honour. He could also be viewed at Madame Tussaud's waxworks (and is still exhibited there today). Later, in the 1930s, there was even a Canadian mountain range named after Scouting's Founder.

A good while after his death, there exists today an estate in Colchester with numerous roads named after Scouting connections, for example Gilwell Close and Brownsea Road.

'Scout' and 'Boy Scout' have also been used to name roads, even locomotives and lifeboats. The images on the next few pages, however, are mainly places with a Scouting and/or Baden-Powell connection.

Gilwell Park, near Epping Forest, Essex, was a run-down estate that was purchased for the movement in 1919. Its previous owner had been William Gibbs, a poet and inventor; perhaps best known for inventing Gibbs' Dentifrice (toothpaste). It became a training school for Scoutmasters and a campsite for Scouts, particularly those from London's poor and crowded East End. Be it the 1920s or today, Scouters from all over the world come to Gilwell to visit, train and camp. Baden-Powell and his family often camped at Gilwell; indeed, Baden-Powell kept his 'Eccles' caravan there permanently.

Baden-Powell House took a long time to come to fruition. This was partly due to the hard times of the war and post-war era. At a cost of £500,000 to build, it was opened by HM The Queen in July 1961. The architect was Ralph Tubbs, who had earlier designed the Dome of Discovery for the 1951 Festival of Britain.

Above left: A modern view of the Wimbledon windmill.

Above and right: Baden-Powell at Pax Hill, his Hampshire home in the village of Bentley. Today it is a nursing home.

~ GREETINGS FROM ~
GILWELL
PARK

Above and left: The Scout Association has resided at Gilwell Park since 2001. The Chief Scout is seen here laying the foundation stone to the new Scout Association office built at Gilwell.

Opposite above: A Gilwell wood-badge course, with Baden-Powell present. This one of 1927, like many others, was authorised to be run outside of Gilwell Park.

Opposite below: The White House Gilwell Park. Photograph depicts Wood Badge course participants and trainers, May 1968.

Above: Interior of Baden-Powell House which was opened in July 1981.

Right: In 1967 the ten Scout Laws were revised and reduced to seven.

Opposite above: Sculpting Don Potter's statue of Baden-Powell.

Opposite below: Baden-Powell House in 2007. The Statue of Scouting's Founder is thought to be London's only granite statue.

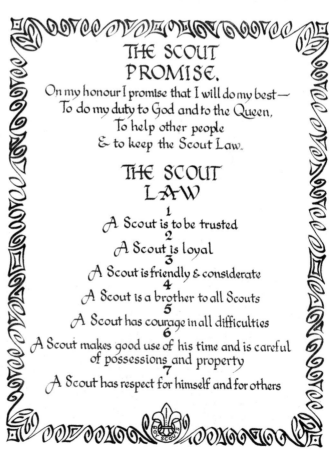

THE SCOUT PROMISE.

On my honour I promise that I will do my best —
To do my duty to God and to the Queen,
To help other people
& to keep the Scout Law.

THE SCOUT LAW

1 A Scout is to be trusted
2 A Scout is loyal
3 A Scout is friendly & considerate
4 A Scout is a brother to all Scouts
5 A Scout has courage in all difficulties
6 A Scout makes good use of his time and is careful of possessions and property
7 A Scout has respect for himself and for others

Baden-Powell's grave.

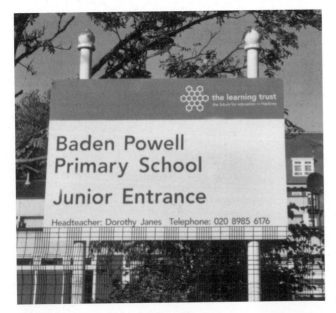

Left and below: Gone but never forgotten.

seventeen

Magazines and Comics

The first Scout paper for the movement was published in April 1908. Priced at 1d and called *The Scout*, it was a typical boys' comic and was intended to reach out to a wider audience than just signed-up Scouts. It suffered early criticism of being too commercial. It was read with awe, however, as it was the chief way Scouts from across Britain – and soon the Empire – could not only read words penned from Baden-Powell's own hand, but see how others were faring. There was great competition and rivalry among the earliest troops, and many couldn't wait to see their name mentioned as a newly registered troop.

Adult leaders would have to wait a little longer for a magazine. It came in the guise of the monthly *Headquarters Gazette*, first published in July 1909. It later became *The Scouter* and then *Scouting*. For many decades these magazines were a common sight on the shelves of newsagents across Britain.

Baden-Powell wrote regularly for the early magazines, and also for national newspapers, but many local Scout Associations (and Scout Groups) produced their own efforts too.

The *King's Scout,* a magazine for south-west London Scouts, was proud to publish a photograph of Baden-Powell's new wife in 1912.

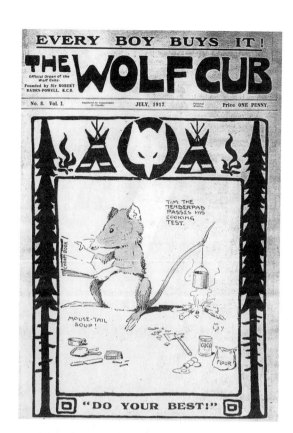

This national comic did not last many years compared to *The Scout*.

In the 1960s, mouth-to-mouth resuscitation was a very modern method for Scouts to learn.

The Scouter, 1962.

Other local titles published by Tempus

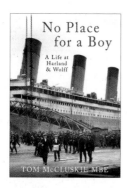

No Place for a Boy
TOM MCCLUSKIE

For boys growing up in Belfast, the great shipbuilding yards offered the opportunity of employment and career advancement. Famous ships like the RMS *Titanic*, and *Southern Cross* were built on Harland &Wolff's berths and slipways. Now the old shipbuilding yards lie derelict, victim to the changing nature of British industry.

978 0 7524 4216 7

Camping for Boys
H.W. GIBSON

Do you know how to make a camp bed, test the freshness of an egg or light a match when there is nothing to strike it on? First published in 1913, *Camping for Boys* was an indispensable guide for any young boy wanting to make the most of the great outdoors. With sections on games for a rainy day, first aid, cooking, organisation, leadership and discipline, this valuable little book will help big kids to regain their youth.

978 0 7524 4311 9

101 Things for a Boy to Make
A. C. HORTH

There are few boys who do not wish to make useful things, and it is for those boys who are on the lookout for suitable occupation that this book has been compiled. Whether it be a Spring Operated Toy Machine Gun, a Garden Swing or a Hot-Air Balloon, this invaluable book, originally published in 1928, captures the fascination and contiual pleasure of making things for the active boy.

978 0 7524 4261 7

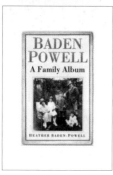

Baden Powell: A Family Album
HEATHER BADEN-POWELL

So begins the story of one of the world's most remarkable father-figures, as told by his own daughter. Quietly, and little affected by the continual hero-worship which surrounded him, Robert Baden-Powell is introduced, the father of the Scout Movement. This often humerous and touching biography, spanning more than half the globe, is both a family story and a public one, uniquely told and extensively illustrated with previously unseen material.

978 0 7509 4441 0

If you are interested in purchasing other books published by Tempus, or in case you have difficulty finding any Tempus books in your local bookshop, you can also place orders directly through our website

www.tempus-publishing.com